Adam lived in a calm small village with his family and a small dog. The dog was the closest friend to Adam. Adam used to feed and bathe the dog every day. He used to take the dog with him everywhere.

Every morning, the dog accompanied Adam to the train to go to his school in a nearby village. All through the way, the dog took care of Adam and defended him from naughty boys or some other dogs guarding the farmers' houses all through the road.

One day the dog accompanied Adam to the train, where many crowded people were trying to get on the train. The dog pushed Adam inside the train and secured him a place.

The train moved and left the station. The dog was very stressed because he could not leave the train. He tried to get off the train, but he could not because of the conflicting crowds blocking the door. So, jumped quickly out of the window.

The moving train hit the dog and cut his tail. The dog cried and asked for help, but nobody helped him. So he ran away and disappeared. Adam did not see what happened and thought the dog would return home safely as usual.

When Adam returned in the afternoon on the same train, he did not find the dog waiting for him. Adam cried and thought that his dog had had an accident and died. He felt deeply sad.

When he arrived home, Adam told his parents about the accident, and they were all sad and sympathetic with Adam. All the family searched for the dog, but they did not find him anywhere.

Adam refused to eat any food and wanted to go out again to search for the dog. When he tried to open the door, he found the dog in front of him bleeding from his behind part and holding his separated tail in his mouth.

Adam and his parents took the dog immediately to the surgical vet and explained what had happened. The doctor asked many questions about the accident. When... where...how???

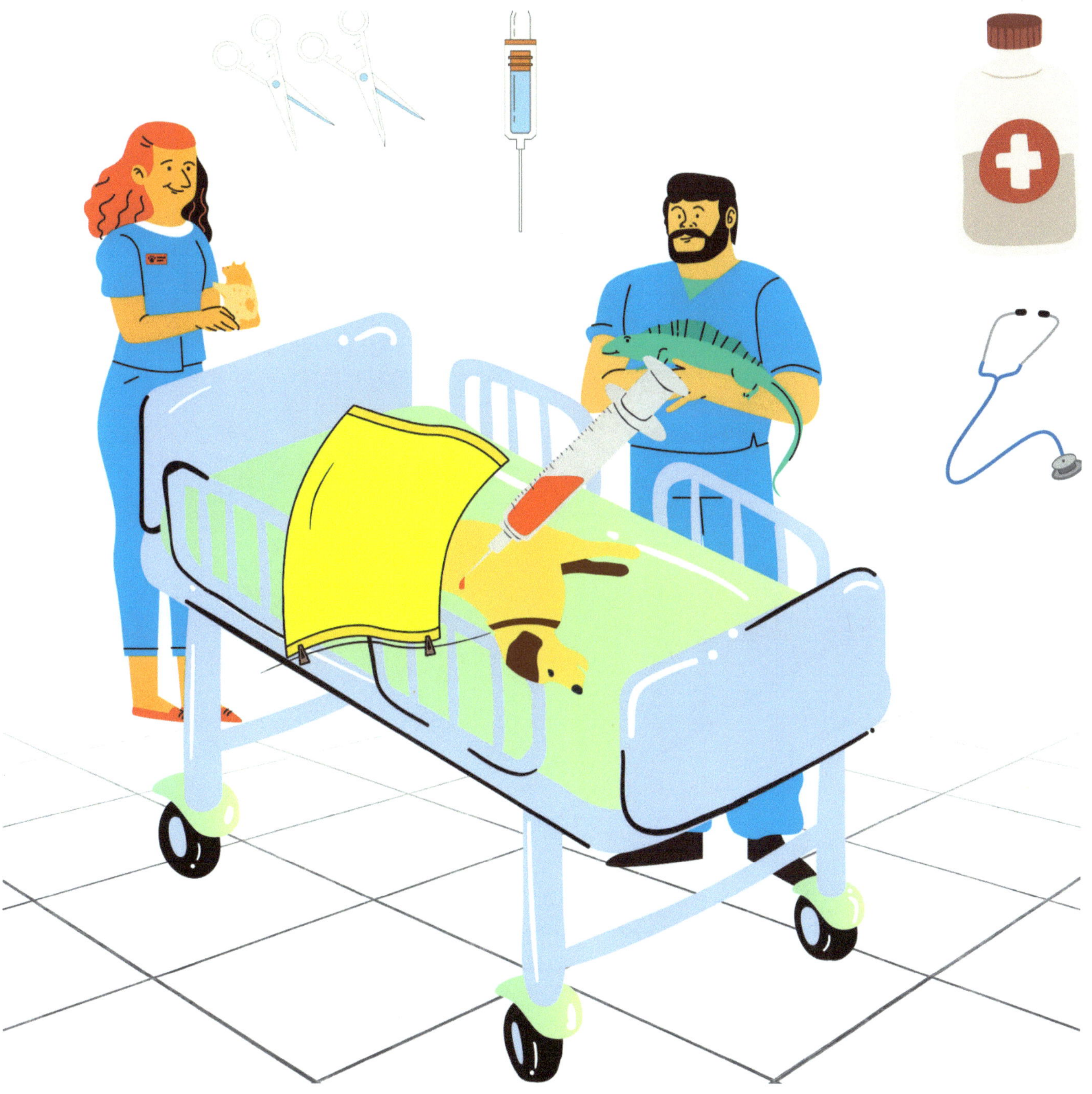

The vet said it is a scarce case. I do not know
if I will succeed. It depends on the vitality of
the living cells in the cut tail and the dog's
body.

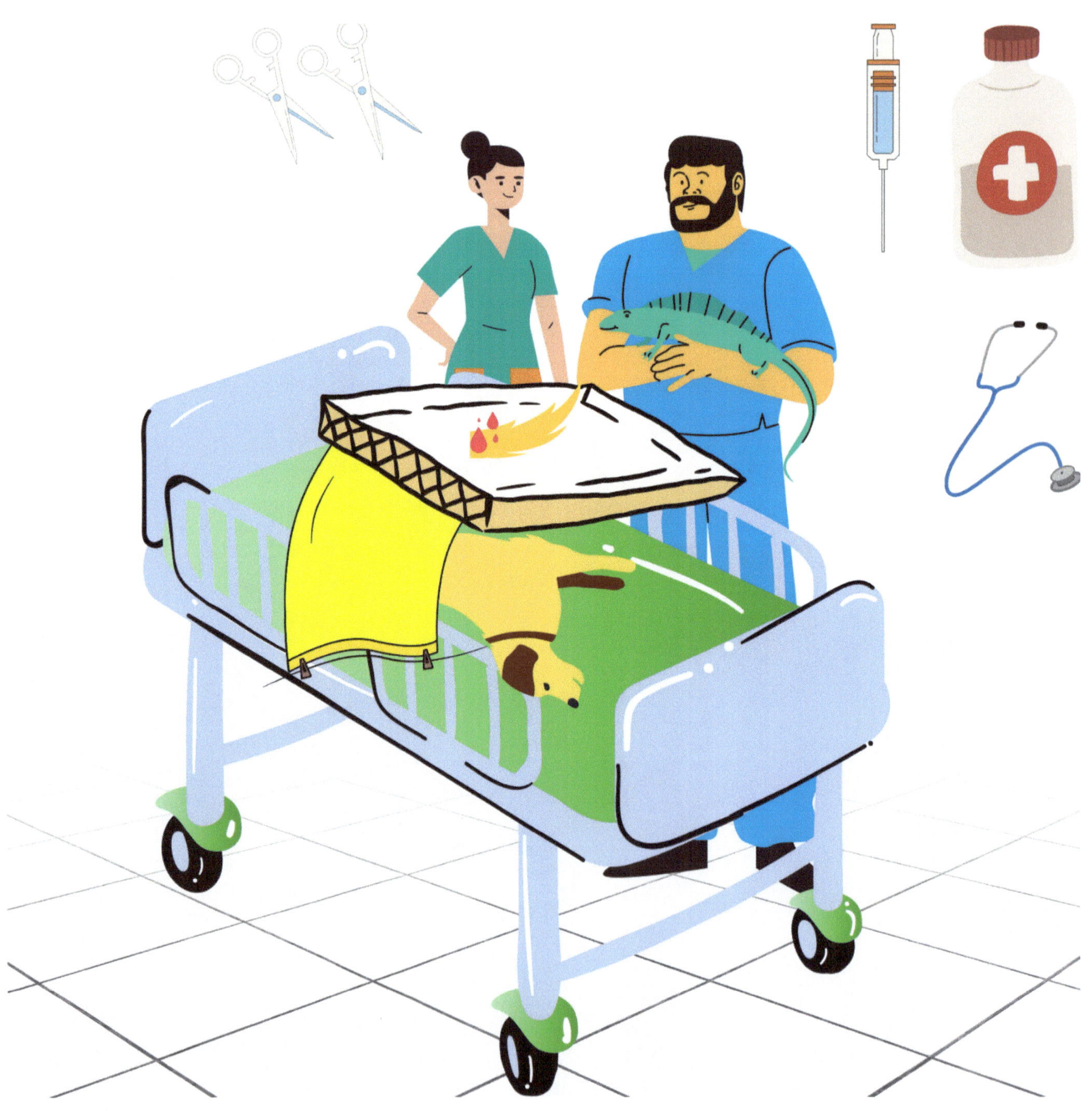

The doctor entered the dog in the surgery room. After a long hard work and with his assistant, they could put in place the separated tail

The doctor got out of the surgery room and said, "I think
we have succeeded. We attached the tail to the body and
we tested the dog's blood running in his Tail. We also
made some tests that dog nervous system is feeling and
controlling the tail now.

The doctor got out of the surgery room and said, "I think we have succeeded. We attached the tail to the body and we tested the dog's blood running in his Tail. We also made some tests that dog nervous system is feeling and controlling the tail now.

The doctor got out of the surgery room and said,
"I think we have succeeded. We attached the Tail
to the body and we tested the dog's blood running
in his tail. We also made some tests that dog
nervous system is feeling and controlling the tail

Adam asked again: "As you correctly have conducted the surgery, can the dog move its tail now. Can I play with him as usual?. The doctor said quickly: "No Adam not right away."

Then the doctor explained that living cells need to attach and regenerate at the place of attachment, which takes time. Then, the body needs to build muscle around the wound.

Then the doctor explained that living cells need
to attach and regenerate at the place of
attachment, which takes time. Then, the body
needs to build muscle around the wound.

Then the doctor explained that living cells need to attach and regenerate at the place of attachment, which takes time. Then, the body needs to build muscle around the wound.

The dog replied: My tail is my only tool to feel and express my pleasure or gratitude. I am so grateful for your family, Adam and I need my tail to say that. I cannot wait to say it.

Adam said: do not worry about that. You are also giving us much pleasure, my friend. You are part of our family.

Adam said: do not worry about that. You are also giving us much pleasure, my friend. You are part of our family.

Although the dog likes and respects Adam, he could not obey his advice. He feels he wants to move his tail as long as he feels happy and cannot help it.

Although Adam asked the dog to stay in place and never go out under any conditions, the dog felt bored and needed to go out. So asked Adam to accompany him to the train the next day. But Adam refused firmly.

The dog repeated his demand many times,
and Adam refused. So, one day the dog
decided to go out after Adam had left for
school.

The dog ran quickly to see Adam off when he was
taking the train. But while he was running, the
dogs around thought he might be attacking them.
So they surrounded him and tried to hit him.

The dog fell down violently over his back and his tail was seriously hurt again. The tail was completely separated with more fights with the dogs, and the dog bled enormously.

The dog was crying in great pain. But the most hurting feeling was his feeling that he betrayed his friend Adam. He felt ashamed of himself.

So he could not return home again. He took his Tail in his mouth and went to a deserted corner nearby the forest.

When Adam returned home back in the
evening, he did not find the dog. He felt
very upset and tried to search for him
everywhere.

Adam hired somebody to look for the dog in the forest and announced at the tongue of Adam: "Please return home. I will not punish you." But the dog was still afraid and ashamed of himself.

In the forest, some kind birds saw the dog bleeding and unable to find his living, so they decided to help him.

They brought food for him every day, cereals and sometimes fish. The dog felt ashamed again because the birds made him services, and he could not even thank them without his tail.

The dog kept his tail, thinking that he could restore its vitality again. However, the separated tail atrophied, withered, and lost life.

With the passing days, the wound in the place of the cut tail began to heal, and the dog started to feel better. The dog tried to move the small part left from the separated tail.

The dog then decided to go home and apologize to Adam and explain to him that it was an accident.

When the dog returned home, Adam blamed
him for leaving the house. The dog replied that
he just wanted to see him off as usual, but the
other dogs attacked him and hurt him seriously.

"So why you did not return home immediately?", Adam asked. The dog replied: "I was ashamed of myself and I could not forgive myself and was very upset. I will never be able to express my gratitude and pleasure again."

Adam said: "Tail is not the only tool to express your joy. You still can jump and run happily and do good things. Doing is the best way of thinking. And you have done a lot to express your thanking, so do not feel sad for losing your tail. Because your feeling and your doing are still there